FOR JEFF DWYER AND ELIZABETH O'GRADY—
MY IRISH AGENTS extraO'rdinaire
—R.M.

FOR CHERYL, CASSIDY AND GRACE
—R.R.

THIS IS A BORZOI BOOK PUBLISHED BY ALFRED A. KNOPF

Text copyright © 2010 by Richard Michelson
Illustrations copyright © 2010 by R. G. Roth

Visit us on the Web! www.randomhouse.com/kids
Educators and librarians, for a variety of teaching tools, visit us at www.randomhouse.com/teachers

Library of Congress Cataloging-in-Publication Data
Michelson, Richard.
Busing Brewster / by Richard Michelson ; illustrated by R. G. Roth. — 1st ed.
p.   cm.
Summary: Bused across town to a school in a white neighborhood of Boston in 1974, a young African American boy
named Brewster describes his first day in first grade. Includes historical notes on the court-ordered busing.
ISBN 978-0-375-83334-2 (trade) — ISBN 978-0-375-93334-9 (lib. bdg.)
[1. Busing for school integration—Fiction. 2. School integration—Fiction. 3. Race relations—Fiction.
4. African Americans—Fiction. 5. Boston (Mass.)—History—20th century—Fiction.] I. Roth, R. G., ill. II. Title.
PZ7.M581915Bu 2010
[Fic]—dc22
2009022626

The text of this book is set in Bailey Sans.
The illustrations were created using ink, watercolor, and collage.

MANUFACTURED IN MALAYSIA
May 2010
10 9 8 7 6 5 4 3 2 1
First Edition

Busing Brewster

By Richard Michelson

Pictures by R. G. Roth

Alfred A. Knopf
NEW YORK

All summer I've been playing on the school playground with Bryan.
I climb the fence by myself, and Bryan catches me on the other side.

"I'll be back soon, Brewster," he tells me. He runs off with
Jules and Big Earl, but I don't mind. There's plenty to do.
I find a stick and swing it like Hammerin' Hank.

smash!

BAM!

I make believe I'm hitting homers, but it's just Jules throwing a rock
high over my head. Uh-oh. I hope that isn't Miss Evelyn's window.
Miss Evelyn's gonna teach me the first grade at Franklin.

SMASH! BAM! CRASH!

"She's mean," Bryan tells me. "She yells like somebody's always setting off her fire alarm."

He squints his eyes and pretends to put on glasses. "You'll learn to read, if it's over my dead body," he screeches.

Big Earl laughs like he's ready to bust a gut.

Bryan makes fun of everybody. Mama says Miss Evelyn's nice.

When we get back home, Mama's on the stoop waving a letter.
"You boys are going to Central!" she tells us.
Bryan moves away before she can hug him. I don't move away,
but I look at Bryan and I don't hug Mama back.

All night Bryan's punching his pillow.

WHOOSH!

"Central's the white school," he says.

WHOOSH!

"I ain't waking up at six."

"At least I won't have Miss Evelyn," I say.
I squinch up my eyes and circle my fingers to
make glasses.

Bryan doesn't laugh. "Miss Evelyn's nice,"
he says.

I'm up by five-thirty, but Mama's already frying eggs. "Don't you worry, Brewster," she tells me. "You're going to like Central. They've got rooms for art and music and a roof that doesn't leak. There's even a swimming pool inside the building and a real library bursting full of books."

I don't know how to read, or how to swim. But I'm glad Mama's happy.

"Maybe you'll be president someday, Brewster," she tells me. And she looks at me proud, like I already am.

By the time we turn the corner, Jules is already waiting at the bus stop. Bryan drops my hand and runs ahead. The bus turns right at the Jewish cemetery. We pass a bar and then a Catholic church. I can't wait till we get to Central. Maybe I'll learn how to swim. I wish Mama had bought me a bathing suit.

"What's that sign say?" I ask Bryan. There's white people lined up
on both sides of the street.

"Welcome to Central," Bryan answers.

But then I see him give Jules one of his "better don't tell on me" looks.

I didn't even see the rock. I just heard the glass shatter.

Bryan squishes me down under the seat. "Wish we could stay at
Franklin," Bryan says. From down here Franklin seems a million miles away.

There's two policemen standing at the Central door, but inside is the whitest hall I ever saw.

There are brand-new shiny lockers lining one whole wall.

There's even a water fountain and it's making me thirsty.

I'm drinking when somebody shoves me from behind. "Wish your kind all stayed at Franklin," he says.

"We like it right here, Freckle-face." It's Bryan, pushing him back.

Now all the older kids are yelling. One of the cops rushes over.

"Well now, lads," he says, "if it's trouble you're wanting, you can follow me."

If Big Earl were here,

he'd be busting a gut.

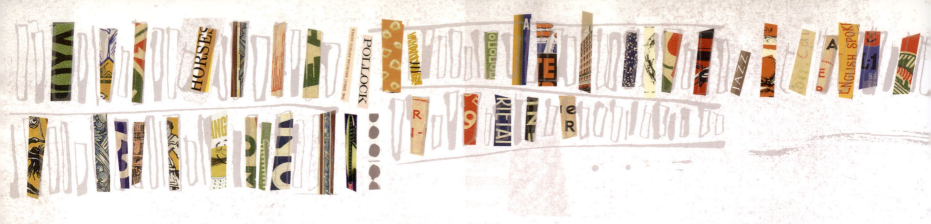

We're spending the whole first day in the library. Bryan says it's called detention, but I don't mind. I've never seen so many books. I find one with a rocket ship on the cover. I turn all the pages and then start again from the front.

I wish I knew what it said.

Miss O'Grady's the librarian. She looks just like Miss Evelyn. "Perhaps you'll be an astronaut someday, Brewster," she says. She brings me a book about the moon landing.

"Mama hopes I'll be president," I say proudly. I feel stupid as soon as I say it. Even I know there's never been a Negro president.

But Miss O'Grady doesn't laugh. "You'll be going from here to Harvard, then," she says, sitting down next to me. "So we'd better begin by teaching you how to read."

Behind her, I see Bryan squint his eyes and pretend to put on glasses. When Freckle-face busts a gut, he sounds just like Big Earl.

Miss O'Grady reads us a book about some man called Kennedy. "Every child deserves an education," she says. "It wasn't long ago that folks didn't want the Irish in their schools. And just because Kennedy was Irish Catholic, people said he'd never be president. But he proved them wrong."

I look over at Freckle-face, but he isn't even listening. He keeps whispering to Bryan and laughing. When the bell rings, they both run out the door.

"I wish you could teach me the first grade," I tell Miss O'Grady.

"You'll do just fine, Mr. President," she says. But she makes me promise to visit her in the library every day.

I'm almost back on the bus when I see Freckle-face standing with his daddy. I start to wave, but he looks away.

"Wish them coloreds all stayed at Franklin," I hear his daddy say.

Mama's waiting on the stoop when we get back home.
"How was your first day at Central?" she asks.

Bryan moves away before she can hug him. He shrugs
and runs off to meet Big Earl at the playground.

I don't want to worry Mama, either, so I give her a big
hug. "I spent the whole day in the library," I tell her.
"Someday I'm going to be president."

Mama looks at me proud, like I already am.

"Maybe tomorrow," I say, "I'll learn how to swim."

Author's Note

Brewster is a composite of many young African American children who, in the 1970s, were bused to previously segregated all-white schools. Segregation generally meant that there were schools for black children and different (better) schools for white children. If an African American child lived near an all-white school, he or she would be forced to travel to a black school, even if it was inferior and far away.

The U.S. Supreme Court had outlawed segregated schools in 1954 (*Brown v. Board of Education*). But even after their ruling, most schools, in reality, were still segregated as, throughout the country, children went to class near their home, and most neighborhoods were not integrated.

In 1971, in an attempt to further integrate schools, the Supreme Court permitted "forced busing." Now, instead of being *allowed* to attend a white school if one was near their home, some black children *chose* or were *forced* to attend a white school, even if none were nearby. To make room for the incoming black students, some white students too had to be bused outside their neighborhoods. This often led to resentment, and occasionally to violence. While much opposition was racially motivated, many blacks and whites honestly preferred that their children attend local schools; parents were unwilling to see their children used as pawns in a social experiment, however worthy. Forced busing failed on many levels, but there is no denying that many black students were provided with opportunities they would not otherwise have had.

In the end, of course, a good education almost always comes down to caring individuals: a loving family that fosters curiosity, and the many librarians and teachers who, like the fictional Miss O'Grady, believe that all children who want to do something important with their lives deserve an equal opportunity.

Brewster dreams of becoming president. Barack Obama was elected the first African American president of the United States in 2008. I wrote this story five years earlier, in 2003. While Miss O'Grady and Brewster's mother might not have been surprised, it never occurred to me while writing *Busing Brewster* that such a historic event would become a reality in my lifetime, much less before the book's publication. My words have taken on a greater resonance than I intended, which is what authors hope for.

In a 2005 speech to the American Library Association, the then Senator Obama gave "an apology for all those times I couldn't keep myself out of trouble and ended up sitting in the library on a time-out." He went on to say that "the moment we persuade a child, any child, to cross that threshold into a library, we've changed their lives forever, and for the better. . . . We all have a responsibility as parents and librarians, educators and citizens, to instill in our children a love of reading so that we can give them the chance to fulfill their dreams."

Maybe even to become president!

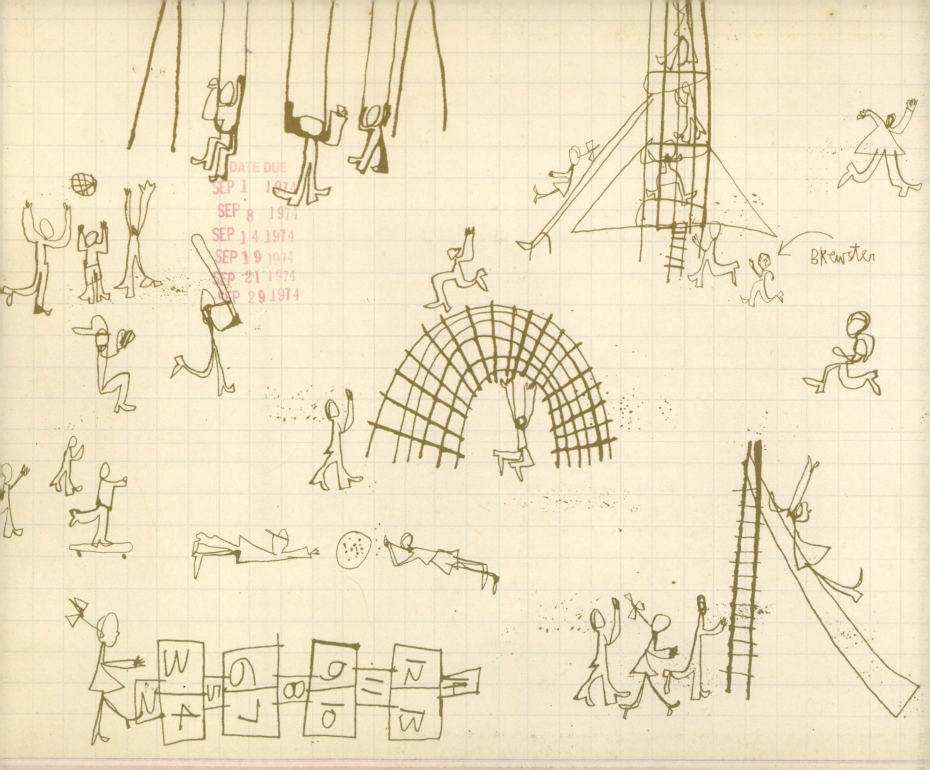

Brewster